MY JOURNEY TO NORMAL
A Miracle Unfolding Before Your Very Eyes

Barbara S. Modena

My Journey To Normal
A Miracle Unfolding Before Your Very Eyes
9781694817969

2nd Edition

DEDICATION

This book is dedicated to my dad, who was one of my greatest providers. My mom, who introduced me to Jesus Christ. My cousin, who treated me like a sister, and my dog Blackie, who was my best friend.

PREFACE

This Book

This book is to let you know that no matter what you have been through, God can bring you out and cause you to move forward to your destiny. From the very beginning, I knew something special was going to happen in my life. It didn't happen in the way I expected, or even the way I wanted, but it molded me and prepared me for such a time as this.

A couple of years ago, my daughter asked, "Mom what were you like when you were not saved?" Those words shocked me. I thought I would never have to go through those memories again but, there it was.

My daughter didn't go to church at the time she asked me that question, but she was nothing like I was at her age. I felt she had the right to know my past, no matter how painful it was to share it.

Her question seemed to open up a forum because my sons started asking me questions and commenting on our past during that same time.

My oldest son told me that he was very upset with me. He mentioned some circumstances in our lives that I was sure I'd been able to hide from him. Situations I wasn't proud of because I hadn't had the confidence or boldness to escape. I told him that I was sorry he had to go through those things because I failed to completely separate us from his stepfather and the destruction, he brought with him.

My children's' questions made me think of all of the other women who didn't consider all of the options they had as they went through some of the things we went through. So, I said to myself, *I will write a book, not just to right a wrong, but to give anyone else who has gone through things that I have a light to guide them through the tunnel.*

My niece and I taking a bath together.
For a little while we both suckled at my mother's breast.

CHAPTER ONE

Reaching for Normal

It's funny how your perspective can change, not only with age but with whom you share your story. How do you know that a beating a day isn't normal when that is all you've experienced? How far away from "normal" does a child get with each verbal lashing or session of abuse?

During my era, it seemed that part of my neighborhood's tradition was to keep their children in line, even if that meant disciplining them each day. It never occurred to me to speak against it, even if shyness didn't have a hold on my tongue. Did I think it was fair? No. Did it make me closer to my mother, who handled most of my physical discipline? No, but it did keep me from other things I had no business doing.

I took the shyness or fear of speaking with me to school. I wanted to answer in class, I wanted lots of friends, I even wanted to tell my parents which

7

extracurricular activities I was interested in, but the words remained locked tight.

As the only child of working parents, with a restaurateur for a grandmother, I didn't ever want for much, but dresses, shoes, and toys were a poor substitute for the affection I was looking for. I had more than most, so wanting even more - like a companion- seemed selfish, but as a child, all you know is what feels good and what hurts. Loneliness hurts.

This picture of my grandmother,
Mrs. Hattie Williams was taken as part
of an article for the Times Newspaper

CHAPTER TWO

My Angel on Earth

My grandmother was a bright spot in an otherwise difficult life. Her name was Hattie Williams, and she had a home restaurant in the neighborhood. She was my maternal grandmother and in a lot of ways, I was more like her than my own mother. She was tall and slightly gruff to others due to her professions, but gentle and firm with me. She was always looking out for me. She would hide me from my parents when she knew they were having a particularly hard day and were looking for someone to take it out on. She would take the foods from my plate that I hated to eat and give them to the dogs under the table when no one was looking.

Mama Hattie saw me as way more than a painfully shy little girl. She was more like a mother to me than my own mother, with whom I had a contentious relationship.

Just waking up each morning was very painful for me, because I knew I would have to face people, and my mother's wrath. I often wondered if some of the things my grandmother and I shared angered my mom. It didn't occur to me then that my mother may have wanted to spend quiet time with my grandmother, be given cakes when no one was looking – as my grandmother did, or be trusted with business secrets. It also didn't occur to me at the time that my mother was only doing what she'd been taught.

There was one particular time when I came home from school with less than stellar, well, let's just call them 'bad' grades. I showed them to my mom in the room that she used as a beauty salon while she was with a client. I think I figured she wouldn't be as harsh if there were witnesses. I was wrong. My mom yelled at me, telling me I was stupid – not for the first time- and said as a woman I wouldn't be any good for anyone and I would be barefoot and pregnant all of my life. The anger and embarrassment proved to

11

be too much for me and after the beating that followed those insulting words, I told her I hated her and wished Mama Hattie was my mother instead of her. It was the only time I saw my mother cry from something I said, but the daily whippings continued.

I began to hate myself, just as I believed my mother did. I began to seriously think that I was worth nothing more than a whipping board because, as a child, I couldn't see that her daily affirmations of my uselessness were a projection of what she thought of herself. I was nothing to her, and nothing to myself. I saw myself through the eyes of hopelessness more often than not. My self-esteem was almost non-existent, and the fourth-grade boys I would have sought solace with didn't want to have anything to do with me.

Thank God.

My shyness caused people to mistake me for being fearful and weak. That impression was far from true, but it brought out those who would take the opportunity to torment those they considered weak. I was bullied as a pre-teen, and my mother came to the school often to settle one dispute or another. I couldn't understand why I got picked on. My hair was always done, and my clothes were homemade but nice. It might have been the fact that I developed faster than the other girls in my class or that my quietness made me a target for kids who wanted to make sure any negative attention stayed off of them. Without a sibling close to my age to share these things with, life was difficult, but not without its saving graces.

My grandmother was one of those saving graces. I know she watched me carefully when I was a child, and she saw me in an entirely different light than anyone else. When I, and the world, saw myself as an extremely quiet, shy and introverted child who seemed terrified to speak, Mama Hattie saw a smart, vibrant young girl with a lot of potential.

My grandmother lived right next door to me and my parents, in a shotgun-style house with a wooden porch high enough off the ground for dogs to lay underneath. It was a place to socialize at the end of the day and if the weather was nice, there would be someone in one of the two chairs watching the kids play at any time of the day

Every so often one or two of the dogs would snap at the ankles of visitors as they climbed the stairs just to give them a little scare.

Rarely could a life insurance collector or salesman get close enough to my grandmother or father because the dogs – not recognizing them - would snap at their heels, giving them a warning that they were not welcome. The children in the yard would laugh while my grandmother or dad would only shout for the dogs to behave themselves.

Every chance I got, I would slip over to her house. Sometimes my mother wouldn't let me go, as if she was exploiting the cherished time I got to spend with Mama Hattie.

Since I was an only child, I was alone most of the time, caught between my thoughts and whatever else I could distract myself with. I had cousins that I got along with well, but since they were at least six years older than me we didn't have much in common. My time with my grandmother was a welcome balm to my inner turmoil. She meant a lot to me. Helping her prepare, serve or clean up around her home restaurant was a blessing because I got to spend time with her. Just being able to sit with her as she let me help her count money in her restaurant made my life brighter.

***

Mama Hattie was a successful entrepreneur in her own right. Her home restaurant was the only place where you could get lunch and it was perfect for the welding factory workers who could get plate lunches delivered to them every day.

Mama Hattie was also the newspaper delivery lady for the three to five-block span near our home. She started working for that newspaper when her grandson went off to college. Although she was well in her late seventies, she would carry fifty to a

15

hundred newspapers on her back, seven days a week. One day at four o'clock in the morning she was stopped by a man who asked her for money. She told the man that she did not carry money on her person. He said okay and left, but the encounter made her wary of going out on her own so early in the morning. She happened to share her fear with a missionary from our neighborhood church. The woman told her to read Psalms 91 every day before going to work. She did, and she felt the fear slip away,

She also began to notice that some of the neighborhood's stray dogs—dogs she would pet, show kindness to, and would leave restaurant scraps for—started to follow her during her deliveries in the mornings. Fifteen dogs ended up following her when she went to work. Two would walk in front of her, one would walk on each side of her, and the other dogs would follow close behind her. She never had any other problems delivering the newspapers. That was my grandmother: Hattie B Williams, the paper delivery lady.

My grandmother had family in Chicago, but I only got to see them during childhood summer visits. My grandmother was my idol. She lived longer than my parents and worked until she was 80 years old. When I left home, I wanted her to come to California to live with me, but she said she wouldn't leave her home.

My grandmother loved to play Butter Negs and Stocks, otherwise known as 'playing the numbers', which was a form of illegal gambling. I didn't know what that was as a child, but I was assigned to count the money. All the quarters, nickels, and dimes were in stacks, and all the bills had to be facing the same way. At my grandmother's house, money was like toys to me. My mother and father didn't play these kinds of games, but that didn't stop my grandmother. Even when I left home, she would call me and ask me which numbers I dreamed about, or what number I saw on TV or in visions, and I would always tell her.

Being away from home, with a family of my own, I was always in need of money. My grandmother would play any numbers I dreamed of and give me the proceeds.

***

Dreams meant a lot to my family, and they were an especially important part of my relationship with my grandmother. Mama Hattie and I had dreams and visions constantly. I thought everyone had them.

It was my grandmother who once called me and said I was going to have a baby girl. I was pregnant with my third child at the time, and I didn't know what it was going to be. She said my daughter would be dark in color, with long legs and long arms. I told my husband we were going to have the girl he wanted, and we were both very happy. I asked my grandmother how she knew from two thousand miles away. She said she saw her in a dream, and I believed her.

My daughter was born with dark skin, long legs, and long arms. Three months later I took her to see my grandmother.

She said, "Yes, just like I dreamed."

That year I was out of a job, so I looked in the paper constantly for anything I would be good at.

I went to sleep and saw a children's home. Everything about it was clear to me: the street names, the building and even the people who did the hiring.

The next day, I looked for a job in the newspaper as I always did, and I saw a company name. I thought the name sounded familiar, but I couldn't place where I had seen it before. When I went to the company and I saw the building I immediately knew it was from my dream from the night before.

I went in with my resume, was interviewed and was hired on the very same day. To God be the glory.

As I got older, I started having nightmares or night terrors. I would dream that I was running and running like someone like the devil was after me, but I wouldn't get anywhere. The dreams got so bad that I had to go to the doctor and ask him for a way to get them to stop so I could get a decent night's sleep.

The doctor gave me sleeping pills that knocked me out so hard that I had to take an upper to stay awake and be able to function during the day. After a few months, I said, "this is not normal. I want to live a normal life."

I see now that I had to break free of those dreams to serve and worship the Lord, my Lord and Savior Jesus Christ, so I could be used to help others.

When I was sixteen my grandmother became the guardian for a baby boy. His mother was one of our neighbors, and she couldn't take care of him, so my grandmother took him in at three days old. He grew up with her, and I was like a surrogate mother.

As she got older he needed a little more supervision, so I had him come stay with me while I was still living at home.

When I went off to college, he had to go back with my grandmother, but he was so rambunctious she had to send him to boarding school.

By the time he graduated from boarding school, I was already in San Diego. He came to visit for a time but eventually moved back home to Tennessee, but before he did, he gave his life to the Lord.

I want everyone to know how Jesus can keep them out of hell and damnation. I truly believe when I gave my life to God at the age of twelve all of those many years ago, God kept me throughout my life of bondage. Thank you, Lord.

Isaiah 30:21: Whether you turn to the right or to the left, your ears will hear a voice behind you, saying, "This is the way; walk in it."

Proverbs. 3:6 In all your ways submit to him, and he will make your paths straight

I still dream, but my dreams are of good things. That's all I can say about that. Hallelujah!

Just me being me even at this age.

CHAPTER THREE

Born Again

Another source of solace was summer. It allowed me to spend more time working with Mama Hattie in the restaurant and on her paper route, but it also lent itself to several opportunities to travel. More often than not, I would be sent to my maternal aunt, but one particular summer I had the opportunity to visit someone else, and it was life-changing.

By now you can tell that I was an awkward child looking for approval. It was painful at times to reach for things that remained out of my grasp. I could play the piano, but at concerts, I would always miss a note or two. I took dance classes but always danced in the back. I ran for queen in different contests but always came in second best. Hah! I asked myself, "what is the purpose of all of this? What is my purpose?" Until one day, during a weekend camp, it all became clear.

When I was twelve, I took a trip to Sedine Bible Camp in Tennessee. It was only a weekend trip, but it changed my life forever. The camp was both exciting and scary since I was away from my immediate family and surrounded by children close to my age. It was something different, and the slightly different environment evoked a certain amount of vulnerability in everyone.

One night the counselors turned out all of the lights, they said a prayer and asked if anyone wanted to accept Jesus in their heart. I raised my hand with other campers and was led in the prayer to receive Jesus Christ in my heart. I felt different almost instantly. Towards the end of the camp, one of the counselors came up to me and said, "You are different from the other children who attended camp this year. There is something special about you, and I'm glad you accepted Jesus into your heart." I understood what he meant because I knew God was calling me to Himself.

I came home and told my mother that I had asked God to come into my heart. She said, "How do you know God came into your heart?"

I said, "Because I don't feel the same as I did before I went."

She asked, "How do you feel now?"

I told her I didn't know, but I hugged her as tears flowed down my face. Hugging her was so much easier than telling her of the depression and other things I'd been doing and going through. I did not want to tell her that I had been cursing, and hanging out with a girl who constantly tempted me to skip school so we could go to her mother's job at a hotel on the other side of town, just to sit in the lobby and eat candy all day.

After camp, I told my friend that I could not curse nor could I skip school anymore. I lost her as a friend, but I didn't feel lonely because God was with me from that day forward.

CHAPTER FOUR

My Mother's Spiritual Life

My mom was the first person to introduce me to the church. We only lived about five blocks from our church. At age three I remember going to church 3 to 4 days a week. I attended Watchnight service every year, Sunday school, junior choir practice, Bible study and church meetings with my mother. My mother wore big feathered hats to church and sang in the choir. Our pastor and his wife would come to our house on Sundays to eat dinner. My mom loved the church and her pastor and First Lady. Sometimes when the pastor came over, he would sit down with his feet on my mother's white couch. I thought to myself *I can't even go into the room and he has his dirty shoes on the couch*. Haha.

Saturdays the First Lady would get her hair done by my mother at my grandmother's house because my mother was the neighborhood hairdresser.

On holidays she would stay up all day and half of the night doing hair. I pledged never to become a hairdresser.

The teachers at my school loved my mother. She would go to all the PTA meetings, and she made me cookies and lunches that would be forfeited to the teachers because I didn't really like what my mom made for me. When I was having trouble in the sixth grade, she hired my sixth-grade teacher to help me during the summer.

My mom had a gift for pretty things, and it showed in our home. When I was in the eleventh grade my dad built her a three-bedroom brick home in the "upper crust" part of town, away from my grandmother. It broke my heart, but my mom didn't seem to notice. She loved to decorate it and I considered her a good interior designer. I guess, wanting to share something she loved with me, she asked me to pick out the towels to go into the bathroom and kitchen. I did my best, but she said it was all wrong. I loved my mother, but I just couldn't ever seem to please her.

The constants in my young life were whippings for things I may or may not have done the previous day, Jesus, who made my days better, overwhelming shyness and daydreams of leaving town by way of scholarships to college.

I'm not trying to paint you a picture of a childhood without laughter, moments of joy, or memories full of happiness. They were there. They count because the mere fact that I accepted Jesus into my heart gave me more joy than I'd had before then. It made me happier knowing I was special to Him and caused me to laugh when He spoke softly in my ear.

My mother and father taught me that hard work, education and church-going would carry me a long way and it has. The memories of them remain in my heart. At times I still find myself with their words on my lips. My relationship with my mother, once I got married, changed. She treated me more like an adult and my perspective of her and life grew.

When I came back home, two months pregnant with my first child my relationship with my mother shifted from mother/daughter to two people who had respect for one another.

We had our challenges as her mood swings became more frequent, but she nearly demanded that I stay by her side.

For ten months I was at her beck and call while waiting for my husband to come back from Vietnam and trying to care for myself as best I could so my baby would be healthy. By the time I had my baby our relationship was closer than it had ever been. A few months later I discovered why.

My mother had been silently battling cancer and was losing. I don't know whether she didn't know until it was too late or just didn't tell us.

It took six months from the diagnosis she shared with us for it to eat away at her body. She never shared her sickness with me, but looking back, the degeneration of her mind and emotions make more sense.

I never remember her being happy, even with all we had. I knew she suffered from some discomfort in her body. At the time I thought it was just minor ailments that we all go through. It didn't occur to me until recently that she could have been fighting this disease for years.

The last day of her life I went to her bedside and I said, "I am going to be fine. You don't have to worry about me." Then I began to pray. She looked at me like it was the first time she saw me. She began gasping for breath, then passed away.

No matter what demons she was wrestling with, my mother introduced me to God, and for that, I will be forever grateful.

My uncle Joe was the only brother my mother had. He lived in another city, but he would come to visit my grandmother, my mother and me every chance he got. I loved my uncle. He had one of his artist friends paint my portrait when I was three years old. It hung on the wall in our home and was passed down from family member to family member for years.

I also had two cousins that I considered brothers because they were the only children related to me that I was close to. Mickey was my Uncle Joe's son and was six years older than me. He lived with my grandmother for a while and decided to make a career of working as a U.S. Postal worker. He was always there to lend a hand and even helped me financially every time I came back to my hometown.

My cousin Sonny, my mother's sister's son, was also close to my heart. Since he was twelve years older than me, I only have one picture of him. It is the one of him posing with my parents and dog Blackie. I hold that picture just as close as I do the china doll he sent me. I was in the fourth grade when he went into the service. He sent me a doll in traditional marriage dress, and after over 50 years I still have that doll. I never saw him again after I got married, but whenever I look at my doll I consider his kindness and how much I miss him.

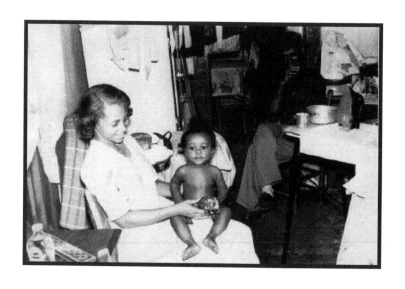

Showing me off

CHAPTER FIVE

Not A Daddy's Girl

My father was a slim, brown-skinned man with straight salt-and-pepper hair. He looked European but we all knew he was 100% black man. *Haha.*

My first memory of my father was of him standing in a home he had two doors down from my grandmother. He always had other men around him. They were always listening to him talk about his stories regarding how he would go hunting in the woods. My dad had hunting dogs and would take them hunting for rabbits and deer every week. One day he came back from hunting and said, "Those no-good dogs couldn't find nothing." It was just so funny to me because now he would have nothing to tell his fellows that night.

My father was a welder, working across the street at a foundry that later gave him Black Lung. I remember my dad working hard and giving me and my mother anything we ever thought we wanted. The

33

neighbors thought we were rich, but I never thought we were any different from them because we were all living in the same neighborhood. I thought we were all rich.

My dad had the respect of all the men in the neighborhood. There were about three or four blocks of us neighbors who knew each other. My dad was a bit of a loan shark 'Booger Bear'. Since his job allowed him to make a decent amount of money, he often had money when others in the neighborhood had run out. He always kept two or three hundred dollars in his pocket.

My parents had a strained marriage. Theirs was not a passionate and romantic marriage. I never saw them look or touch each other affectionately. It was convenient for both of them. My father had been divorced for twenty years before he met my mother. He was almost ten years older than her. My mother wanted to be married and have children and he was a man of means and well-spoken of around town so he was a good candidate. They both had very

34

independent lives. I felt like I was their one connecting variable. The one thing that brought them home--not necessarily for my sake—they just wanted to be in the vicinity so they could say they were doing their job. Our house wasn't huge, and with three people it should have been cozy but in actuality, it was very lonely.

What is normal? Living with my mother and father, with my grandmother next door, was normal for me. So, when I grew up and saw three, four or five children in a house and never saw their father, that was not normal for me. Sometimes I would ask, "where is your father?" Most of the time they would say they didn't know. So, I was confused. It just didn't seem normal. Having a mother, father and grandmother that were always around – even if they were just in the next room - was all I knew. It was one of the reasons why I cried for days when we moved to the house my dad had built for my mom. It felt like a piece of me was missing even though my grandmother was only ten miles away.

I think my father cheated on my mother, but I never knew for certain. However, we had every materialistic thing we wanted, and he always came home at night with bags of food for my grandmother to cook with when we were still living next to her. During Christmas, the tree was filled underneath with presents. I thought it was normal for everyone in the neighborhood to have the same.

As I got older, I would have more and more friends say "I never knew my father," or "I can't stand my brother." All these things that I would never say were the norm for my friends. There were many things I didn't notice in my sheltered world.

I was playing out front with two small children, not much smaller than myself, but because, at the very mature age of nine, I was the older one, when they decided to jump off the porch, I took it upon myself to catch them. It didn't go so well. Their momentum sent me stumbling backward, and I hurt my ankle. Knowing he was closest, I called for my dad using every bit of alarm a young child would use when trying to get a parent's attention. That didn't go so well either.

"You shouldn't have been doing that in the first place. You're no bigger than they are," were the first words out of his mouth as he looked at me lying on the ground after hearing what landed me there. The fact that I was clutching my ankle with tears rolling down my cheeks seemed to be lost to him. I don't believe I would have cried for as long as I did, but the nurturing I needed at that moment was denied to me and I swear it made my ankle hurt even more.

His reprimand missed its target. It went right over my head and swung around to pierce me in the heart. Instead of making me sad, its sting made me angry.

"You don't love me," I said in a huff, expressing my displeasure at his failure to meet what I thought was an obvious need.

What I didn't expect was his refusal to be shamed by his nine-year-old little girl.

"I sure don't."

I had no response. I was completely and utterly dumbstruck. I can't say it was a complete shock. I'd heard more than once that my father loved my older half-sister more than any of his girls; those from his first marriage, or me from his second marriage.

My dad had three children from a previous marriage. All three of the children were in their twenties by the time I came along. My arrival came at the same time as my niece, my older half-sister's child and we both suckled at my mother's breast because my half-sister took ill.

I never met my half-brother, who was already fighting in the Korean war when I was born. He didn't come back from that war, but every picture I saw of him let me know that he was the spitting image of my dad.

Every now and then my half-sisters would come to visit their dad, his new wife, and child. My mom embraced them as much as they would allow, but I was not to fool myself into thinking that we were close or that they considered me as one of their siblings.

Throughout our adult life I constantly reached out to my older siblings. Some of my efforts reaped the reward of spending time with them and sharing memories over a day of shopping and other efforts were in vain. One of my half-sisters said she would try and keep in touch with me if I came to see her. I did so every weekend; driving 45 minutes each way. I thought if I made the effort our relationship wouldn't suffer. It didn't matter that I put in more time and effort. She is family and we are still close to this day

My other half-sister waited until I called her while she was on her deathbed to apologize for her behavior towards me, and for not loving me like a sister. Even though I called her every year without her picking up the phone, I hadn't seen her in a decade. I cried all of that night after hearing her words of apology. I had always loved and respected her as my big sister. I felt cheated out of the time we could have had, but I was happy that she finally acknowledged me as her younger sister.

Now that I think about it, my half-siblings weren't the only ones with issues expressing their feelings. If it weren't for others in the neighborhood telling me how proud my dad was of me, I probably still wouldn't know.

My neighbors would say "He loves you, but he wants you to be a strong woman and not rely on him and his love so much." If I could have been sure they wouldn't have spanked me, I would have looked at them sideways. What kind of sense did that make? All I wanted was to hear him tell me that he loved me.

It's hard to get around the words, even when the deeds say something different. Words are a lot more profound than we think.

As I got older, I stopped looking to him for confirmation of his feeling towards me. I didn't want to hear what he would say.

I remember being molded by both of my parents. I wasn't asked what I wanted to do. I was told what I wanted to do. I can't recall how many times I helped my father do drywall, fix cars, cement walkways or put in a garden.

My dad wanted a boy. I think that was because he lost his son in the war. He taught me so many outdoor activities, I bet I could change a tire or spark plugs faster than some of the boys in my neighborhood and don't get me started on my green thumb. We grew Concord grapes in our backyard, and I learned how to take care of them alongside my dad. My grandmother, who was also a bootlegger, would press them to make wine.

Except for the year I accepted Christ into my life at camp, I went to Chicago every summer to stay with my great aunt Maddie. I would go by train with a traveler's aid attendant. The train ride was delightful. I would look out the windows and see all the different country landscapes. I would see different trees, common grasses, and animals and people going to-and-fro. One of my aunts had a family grocery store called Maddie's family store. I would sit behind the counter watching the people and greeting them as they walked in the door. I also watched them squeeze the bread and bruise the fruit. My aunt would tell them with a smile, "I just went to the market place this morning. Please don't bruise the fruit or squeeze the bread."

My father was well respected in our small community. He was looked up to as a decent and prosperous family man. When I graduated from high school, I overheard him telling his buddies that I, Bobbie Sue, made it to graduation without any scandals, any babies, or anything that would embarrass the family. I heard him say with pride in his voice. "Nobody can say anything bad about her."

It was the best compliment I could have asked for from him. The fact that I overheard him telling others didn't lessen its meaning for me. Quite the opposite. I knew he loved to boast to his friends about his hunting trip and his dogs. Some of his stories were true, and some were sprinkled with half-truths, but when he sat down to talk to his friends whatever he spoke of was something he felt he could boast about.

I had done something right.

My life has taken a few turns, but I still can remember my father's voice and the pride with which he spoke of me that night. It gave me even more reason to watch myself around my father's men so they couldn't say "See, she wasn't what you said she was."

It also reminded me of a few incidences during my childhood that now look different. He may not have been the most affectionate man, but he protected me.

While walking to school, one of my neighbors asked me if I wanted a ride. It was raining, and I said yes, please. I was about thirteen years old. I got in the car and he drove about half a mile. Then he put one hand on the wheel and one hand on my thigh. I was shaking with fear by the time we reached the school, where all the teachers and students stood outside. I hurried out of the car.

When I came home, my mother asked me, "How did you get to school today?"

I knew something was up because she never asked me that before.

I said, "Mr. Dunne Buggy took me to school."

One of my teachers had called my mother; another teacher, who had tutored me the previous summer, told her I came to school in a stranger's car.

She told my dad and I never saw that man again

When I came back home to visit eight years after I had left for California with my second husband, I saw for the first time how other people had lived in other neighborhoods across the tracks. In order for me to get home from the airport, I had to go through a neighborhood that I had never been through before. The houses were huge with flat-top roofs and luxury cars in the driveway. I asked the taxi driver when those homes were built. He said they were over a hundred years old. Then I saw the shotgun houses where my grandmother and we lived before we moved. Our house was still there; it was a two-room place with a back porch and an outhouse. I grew angry when I understood that only a few blocks separated the houses owned by whites and the houses rented by blacks. Even more poignant was the fact that part of the neighborhood was separated by a bridge which people had come to know as 'the hanging bridge' since a number of black boys caught out after dark had been hung from the overhead railing for all to see in the city.

Due to his work at the Foundry for so many years he had to have one of his lungs removed. He lived 10 years with the one lung but died of Black Lung. My father died when I was twenty-four. My second boy was still under a year old, but he would babysit him when I had to go to work.

It took a long time for me to understand that I brought behaviors from my childhood with me all the way into my late adulthood. Only recently did I realize that the need for approval directed much of my life.

God is teaching me to listen closely to His voice and follow him. When I pray I try to ask God each and every day which way am I to go.

Willie Edward Modena
My brother who died in the Korean War

CHAPTER SIX

My Turn

In high school, I had dreams of joining the Peace Corps because I wanted to help people while experiencing the beautiful world God had made. My mother wouldn't allow it, but there was still the hope and dream of college and the independence that would bring me.

I remembered praying to God about going to the college that some of my friends were going to. I didn't get an acceptance letter right away and I remember walking down the street and seeing a church open. I went in and fell to my knees asking God to let me go to college. My family was very big on education, so I wanted to go to college although I was a 'C' student. After I prayed I walked back home and went to the mailbox. There was a letter saying that I had received a full ride to attend a four-year college. A full four-year scholarship to attend a college in Knoxville, Tennessee? I was over-the-moon happy. I asked my mom to look over the letter.

"Mom is this right, does this mean I can go to school now?" She was crying and nodding before I could get all of the words out.

"You have been accepted to attend school in Knoxville."

I gave God all the honor and glory.

At seventeen I went off to college happier than I could ever remember being. Life was full of possibilities, and even though Ms. Shyness followed me around, her chokehold on my tongue had eased some and I was able to make some friends. For once I didn't mind waking up, and I had hope for a better future.

Little did I know that life was about to get more complicated. Instead of finishing college, my boyfriend was drafted into the army. He wanted us to stay together, so he proposed marriage. It's what every young woman wants to hear from her college sweetheart, isn't it?

At nineteen I was still a minor in the eyes of the law; 1969 a woman was a minor until 21. I had to get my mother's permission. All that stood between me and marriage and getting away from that small town in Tennessee forever was her signature. And don't you know it didn't come without paying a steep price.

For days and days, I tried to convince her that this was right for me, that this was what I wanted, that I knew what I wanted, but she refused. I became extremely morose and depressed because the freedom I once thought was so close was moving further and further away. Once I became his wife, in essence, I was no longer her daughter. There was someone between me and her abuse when I came home.

The depression got worse as the brightness of my future dimmed, and the enemy started speaking hopelessness to me. The darkness in my mind and the heaviness of my emotions reached a breaking point the night before I searched the house for every pill I could find. There was no one there to stop me, and there were no last thoughts of inspiration or revelation to keep me from taking them, so with a stomach full of pills, I went to sleep. And then I woke up the next morning feeling better than I had ever in my life. I was a suicide failure, and today I have to say that that was one of the best failures I have ever had. A few days later my mom gave in and sign the paper. Sometimes I think of what my then-boyfriend would have done had he discovered that I'd given up. I also wonder if my mom would have grieved had I succeeded.

It's funny how you don't think of those things at the moment. You can't see anyone around the pain and darkness that surrounds you. It's hard to imagine life and other people going on without you. But thank God in that instance no one had to grieve for me. Instead of my funeral, my family planned a wedding.

I'm not going to go as far as to say that my mom was right in her hesitation to see us married. I had a beautiful child through that union that I would not otherwise have. My children are the special gems of my life, even if I couldn't keep them from being scratched on occasion. It took becoming a mother to understand that with all of my mother's flaws, there was love, there was pride, and there was caring, but whatever had a hold on her kept her from expressing it in a way that I could always receive. I wish I could have understood her type of love then. I would have learned the easy way that abusers recognize abusers.

There were many life-altering events that happened during our marriage. As I've said, I had a child, but what I didn't share was that I was recruited by the FBI as a file clerk during my second year of college. It was a short-lived position because my husband went to war and I went back home after finding out that I was pregnant. It took another ten years before I received my bachelors.

Once I got back home, I started attending the University of Tennessee in Chattanooga. The summer after my first year there I was at my grandmother's house asleep when a woman knocked on my grandmother's door. She said she was canvassing the neighborhood for young black women who were interested in job training for a new government program. My grandmother came to me and told me there was a woman giving away jobs and if I wanted one, I should get up and talk to her.

While talking to the woman I mentioned that I was in college. It turns out that the director of her program had attended the same college. A few weeks later I was working as a job coach where I counseled young men and woman on how to interview for a job. It helped reinforce my love for counseling and built my confidence. It also paved the way for a rewarding career in social work that would begin later in life and that I would enjoy for over fifteen years. That summer, life seemed to be taking a turn for the better.

My husband never really came back from the war. He may have looked like my husband. He may have walked like my husband. Sometimes he may have talked like my husband, but the war had changed the person I knew and loved into someone I barely recognized. He would mentally abuse me daily and in one instance he even pulled a gun on me. It was almost a relief when I received the credit card statement showing the charge for his Hawaiian getaway with another woman. I also found a picture of him and the same woman. He had lived with her during the war.

By the time it was all said and done I almost had less coming out of my marriage than I had going into it.

It took years for me to come to the understanding that the bullet he used to kill his second wife was meant for me. A few days before I left him, we went to a club. When he went to find me a seat I ran into a childhood friend who happened to be gay. He asked me to dance and I accepted because it had been so long since I saw him. When my husband saw us dancing, he came up to us and told us that he would kill us if he ever saw us talking to one another again.

My husband had a phobia regarding homosexuality, and I had just gotten him too close to someone he feared and hated.

Since he was so angry at the club, that night I hid the guns while he was sleeping, and the next night he went around the house looking for them. I felt the volatile energy surrounding him and I know now that he would have shot me. I left the next day. No need to stay around until he killed me.

I filed for divorce and packed up my baby and my things. He married the other woman six months after our divorce. He ended up shooting and killing her four and a half years later. He told people that it was self-defense. No one listened to him, but my high school friends, who knew both of us, told me that they believed that bullet was meant for me. Whether or not that was true, I am grateful to God for keeping his hand over me and my child and staying the hand of the enemy.

I never thought of myself as a woman with big dreams. I loved my family and I wanted to be accepted by my family. I wanted my husband to show me love and I wanted a child that would love me unconditionally.

Faith with works.
This is the dress I had made in hopes
of going to the beach one day.

CHAPTER SEVEN

Out of the Frying Pan

No child, when asked what they want to become when they get older, will tell you they want to be controlled by a narcissistic melomaniac who verbally and physically abuses his family and sets up his wife for sex trafficking. Hopefully, no child will grow up to realize this nightmare is their life when they hit their early adulthood. Mercifully they will arrive at "Normal" early on in life and remain there. For me. It was a long journey to "normal'.

During the last year of my first marriage, I met the man who would change my life forever.

I like the concept of marriage (especially the fairytale version). During my first marriage, the thought of divorce broke my heart until it was clear that my life was on the line.

During my second marriage, divorce was not something I was willing to consider while saying my vows, setting out on a new adventure, watching that adventure turn sour, doing things I never thought I would do, ducking from fists or running for my life. Many people would run to the courthouse and terminate the contract with a signature, but I took my vows to God seriously and I held the covenant I made before God close to my heart. I hoped my second husband would begin to live as he spoke when we were dating. I hoped he would turn to God and listen with a sensitive ear to what God was telling him. I prayed that he would get on his knees and pray for God's forgiveness.

Unfortunately, he got down on his knees in front of another god. One that could be received intravenously and gave my husband an aberration of peace that lasted only as long as there was a chemical reaction within his body. He worshipped a god that took instead of gave; a god that had him bending every spoon I owned in the house. To this day I don't have metal spoons in my home.

I married my second husband almost one year to the day I met him. He seemed to have a great sense of adventure, and he was full of dreams and so was I. Some of those dreams I shared with him, and then I had a few I kept to myself. One of the dreams I shared was to move to California. California, the land close to the ocean, nearly seventy-five degrees every day, and opportunities.

I'd wanted to go to California ever since speaking to my half-sister who lived in San Diego. Two years later I was on my way with husband number two and two little boys.

California, Here I Come.

My husband wanted to follow me because he knew I was leaving my hometown. One of the reasons why I left was because my father died of lung cancer from working at the welding factory for so many years. It was the only well-paying job for black men in that area, and I didn't want my two boys to have to work there. I was also excited to be going to a city with next to no winters. I even had dresses made for myself that were only to be worn at the beach.

So, my second husband and I packed our car and headed for California. On the way, we went to see my niece who lived in Ohio. This was the same niece who nursed at my mother's breast with me. I often thought of her as a sister, rather than a niece since we were the same age. She extended her hospitality toward us for the month and she and I were closer than ever after that.

The first time I saw the ocean I was in awe. While I lived in the deep South, I had only seen a small lake, but I knew someday I would live by an ocean, so I had clothing made to wear to the beach before I ever even got close.

The ocean calms me and gives me a sense of well-being. Looking at water that stretches out as far as the eye can see is incredible to me. It's like unending peace. Walking along the beach or sitting on the beach looking at the foaming white waves are the best.

Once we arrived in California, my husband started hanging around men who had also come from my hometown. Either their influence was very strong, or he wasn't the man I thought he was. He was happy to follow their ideas of the ideal marriage, but it didn't bode well for me, because with that group of men, the

roles of marriage were reversed. The women were the breadwinners and the men stayed home with the children. It might have been a little better if they took care of the children while they were home with them, but I was taught not to be greedy.

My first job? Finding enough food for the week without getting caught.

I knew it was wrong. It wasn't the illustrious career I'd trained for. Actually, I'd worked for an organization whose main pursuit was to prosecute people who did what I was doing. My five-finger discount career escalated from there to selling pieces of my dignity that weren't easily forgotten.

CHAPTER EIGHT

Things We Tell Ourselves We Deserve

When you live in constant sin, it's hard to believe that God will come to your rescue when you call. It's hard to imagine that He is still there waiting for you where you left Him. The enemy doesn't have to work hard to deceive you into believing that because of your sins, you deserve every bad thing that happens to you.

I didn't think the Lord would hear me; I was so deeply ensconced in my sin. But God, knowing I would be in this place each night still came to my rescue. He saved me, knowing that I believed if I repented, my children and I might starve to death. It was a sin I wasn't ready to get out of because it kept a roof over my head and food in my children's bellies. Knowing all of this, He still heard my cry and saved me.

One night while I was about the business of hospitality and customer service, street corner style, a man drove up to me and said he wanted a service only I could provide. He opened his door for me to get in, but I waited. We were always told to get paid before we got in anyone's car.

The man pulled out a knife and said that he would kill me if I didn't get into the car. He put the knife to my throat and told me to get into the back seat. I did what I was told, hoping I would be allowed to live through whatever he was about to do and see my children again.

He saw my purse then. It was the purse my aunt had given to me. It was red and shaped like an envelope with the letters K-I-T-T-Y. engraved on a gold nameplate. The man looked at me and said "Oh. You're Kitty right?"

I didn't know what answer he was looking for, so I decided to be agreeable.

I said yes.

He seemed to like that and wanted to talk. So, with the knife still to my neck, I talked to him, hoping this wouldn't be the last few minutes of my life.

After he finished with me, he said, "Well Kitty, you can go now."

I ran out of the car, leaving my purse, just thankful he didn't kill me that night. It took a long time for me to admit to myself that I was raped. I coped with it by telling myself it happened to someone else. In those dark moments when I couldn't convince myself it didn't happen to me, I told myself I deserved that treatment because I was out there.

I didn't deserve that type of treatment no matter what I was doing as a profession. What I needed, and got, was mercy. Even in the midst of my sin.

***

The spiritual and mental war I battled became harder every day.

How was I going to feed my kids and take care of them in a place so far from everything I knew?

I had an abortion shortly after I had my second son. My husband went to jail, which was common by then. I met a guy through other friends. We dated a few times, but the relationship didn't last. I found myself pregnant with a child. A male child. I was afraid to keep the baby because I just had a baby. I didn't know what my husband would do if he found out I was pregnant. After the abortion, I found out that the man I was dating was a candidate ministry. I never told him I was pregnant with his son.

I have repented and God has forgiven me and though there remains a scar, I have been fully healed. That's why I can counsel women who have gone through abortions and let them know that repentance and forgiveness are real and it does heal completely.

I know that none of this is worth my soul or being separated from God for eternity. He loves me that much. He loves you that much.

My home away from home in Tennessee

CHAPTER NINE

A Mother's Work is Never Done

One night during our time in Hollywood I went out to get a Christmas tree for the boys. It was one of the many nights my second husband left me and my boys alone. I asked a neighbor to check on them while I was gone. While I was out, my first husband came to the house and took both boys. He called the Los Angeles branch of Social Services and reported that I had abandoned my children. They took my second son and my first husband took his son back to Tennessee with him. When I got back to the house with the tree the neighbor said there was nothing she could do. My first husband had papers from the Tennessee court saying that I'd left town with our son without telling him. Since he was well-liked at the time in the city, they were more than happy to do his bidding.

I couldn't believe it. I spent most of that night in a panic and a daze. I didn't know what I could do to get my children back. Over the next few days, I made call after call, including to family services, but they were no help.

After a few months, I'd raised enough money for an airplane ticket and went back to Tennessee. I got a job at a television station as a PBS program director and started the procedure of getting my first son back. They said I had to have my own two-bedroom apartment and a job, and I acquired both. I worked hard for months, and just when I procured everything I needed to get custody of my son back, his father shot and killed his wife.

It was a bittersweet ending to a traumatic time in our lives. The courts automatically gave me my son back since my ex-husband couldn't keep custody of our son while he was serving a prison sentence, regardless of whether it was self-defense or not.

My second son was still in Los Angeles. I spoke with him every day while I was in Tennessee. He was only three years old, and I cried each day he was away from me. There was one day I called him and he said something I didn't understand. It took a moment for me to realize that he was speaking Spanish. I asked him what he said but he kept speaking Spanish.

When the group home mother came on the phone, she told me that my son had been staying with a Spanish-speaking family. My son spent several months with that family before he and the social worker flew to me in Tennessee. I was elated and excited to see my son again. I arrived at the airport early, hoping to catch first sight of him. I looked around as I paced the area where we were to meet, getting more anxious by the minute.

During one of my passes, I saw a woman walk passed me with a little boy. I gave them little mind because they were all speaking Spanish. It was only when the boy stopped and grabbed my dress, interrupting my forward progress, that I really looked at him. It was my son, speaking Spanish and saying, "Madre, Madre."

I almost fainted with joy before scooping him up and holding him close. I had my two boys back with me.

North county Condo
A miracle from Los Angeles to San Diego

CHAPTER TEN

God's Goodness

Close to a year after my boys and I moved back to Los Angeles our apartment complex caught on fire.

We lived on the top floor of a four-story apartment building, which had steps on the outside that lead to each floor.

A man whose girlfriend lived on the ground floor started the fire in a fit of rage. The girl died, and the rest of the tenants were left to find a way out of the building. The fire made its way up the walls and inside the stairway, leaving us with little choice of how to get out.

We were still debating whether we had enough time to make it below when my oldest son ran and jumped out of our fourth-floor window to the ground below. The terror that ran through me almost caused my heart to stop. I thought surely he'd broken something, but he jumped to his feet and yelled. "I'm fine. I'm all right Mama."

God saved my son!

My boys and I were sitting on the street after that with no place to go, but we were befriended by a pair of actors who took us in for a week until we connected with the Red Cross and were placed in a hotel for another week. My husband was still in the picture but chose to stay somewhere else.

Earlier in the year, I'd made a trip to San Diego for a jazz festival and I saw how inexpensive rent was in the 80s. It seemed like the best place to escape to in light of my situation.

On the bus on the way to San Diego the second time, I sat next to a woman sheriff who was planning to move out of town. She asked me if I wanted her two-bedroom condo. I gladly said yes. It was a fabulous condo. We moved in the next week.

God is good.

My husband chose to stay in Los Angeles to 'finish some business,' I guess I was better at stealing than he was. I'd definitely had more practice. He ended up in jail for three years, which would begin a revolving door that brought him in and out of our lives.

My sons and I received three years of peace. No walking on eggshells, stealing food or doing things I couldn't do in front of my children. I was able to get a night job so I could take them to school in the morning and pick them up in the afternoon. I went back to school and finally acquired my B.A. in Behavioral Science. It was one of the best times of our lives.

That first year in the condo I put my boys in camps for the summer. They learned how to swim and play tennis.

I later enrolled them in karate classes at the Naval Base. I wanted them to be social boys in the neighborhood and learn how to defend themselves since there was no man around them to protect them or teach them how to protect themselves. The teacher came to pick them up and bring them home. One day, he let them out of the car across the street from our condo. A drunk driver ran up on the sidewalk and hit

75

both of my boys. The older boy pushed the younger boy to the side, and he received the brunt of the oncoming car. They both had to go to the hospital with major injuries. By pushing his brother out of harm's way, the older boy got most of the injuries, but God's hand was upon them. They were able to make a full recovery and while my oldest was still in the hospital the Chargers and Shriners came to visit him, calling him a hero.

After being in prison for several years my husband joined us in San Diego. We had a baby girl. The condo was being sold, so we moved further north.

My youngest child, a girl, was born ten years after my youngest son. When she was still a baby, she contracted a very high fever. My husband was at home at the time and I told him to come into the room with the child and see how God would cast down that fever from our daughter. I put my hand on her head and I brought my head down over her body. I told my husband to put his hand on her head where I had just touched her, and he did. He said her head is cold I said now put your hand on her feet and he did. I said her feet are hot. So, I ran my hand over the rest of her body down to her feet then I told my husband to feel the rest of her body down to her feet and he did so. He told me her feet were cold and I told him that God did that.

I said, "God is a healer."

I praised God and I wanted my husband to believe as I did. I don't know if he ever did. He admitted once that he did believe, but he enjoyed doing what he was doing and wasn't ready to change.

After being out of the church for ten years, my heart was in shambles and sick from not having the fellowship with the saints. I was in Tennessee trying to get to California back in the seventies, and when I got to San Diego, I did not find a church until I started working in Mira Mesa.

One day at work, some friends asked, "Why don't you come to my church?"

I decided to take them up on their offer one Sunday. When I attended, I found out it was a Pentecostal church. They were clapping their hands singing out loud and women were preaching. I had never heard of such a thing. The drums were playing, and all of the sudden water was running down my face. I didn't know why I was crying; I just felt so good. Better than I had in many years. I couldn't wait for Sundays so I could be in church. It was a place of peace and refuge. Of being at church.

One Sunday a missionary told me and all of the girlfriends I worked with who also belonged to the church, to come to Bible study during the week.

It had been so long since I'd been in church during the week, I could hardly imagine going to church on a weekday, but I went.

There was a church down the street having a revival and when the young women attended, they were asked if they wanted to receive the Holy Ghost. They answered "Yes." They were baptized and came up speaking in tongues, as they were immediately filled with the Holy Spirit. I was shocked and stood there with my mouth wide open. I was also jealous that I wasn't there to receive Him as well.

I began praying with the group and fell out under the influence of the Spirit. My tongue began to move up and down in my mouth. I told the group that I was speaking to God, but they didn't believe me, so I kept speaking with my mouth closed. I knew the Holy Spirit was dwelling within me and asked God to translate what He had me saying and He gave me that gift as well.

Soon after receiving the Holy Ghost I went to sleep and had a dream that children were falling into a pit of hell. I woke myself up, but the vision continued. The children were on a mountain in a line. There were hundreds and hundreds of children with one behind the other lined up and walking towards a hole in the mountain with fire rising up from it.

I heard a voice saying, "If you don't tell the children about me, they will fall into the pit."

It took a long time for me to connect this dream with the children's books I write, teaching them about the Bible.

***

My son left home when he was sixteen years old because he didn't want to go to church or taking out the trash every day. His basketball coach took him in, and during those months the coach got him a scholarship to Oak Ridge University. After two years my son decided not to go back to school. I was distraught thinking that the biggest chance for his success was lost.

One month after school started, the school was damaged in the biggest earthquake California had had in many years. The school building suffered heavy damage. The dorm rooms he'd been assigned to were flattened, and students lost their lives.

This wasn't the first time God saved my son.

My son just recently told me that when he was young, he drove into a lake and couldn't manage to swim to the top. He said he felt something pull both his arms up until he saw the top of the water. He didn't know how or who pulled him up, but I know.

We had no idea what God was doing, but He blessed us.

At age sixteen, my second son was popular with the kids in the neighborhood and always had them following him. I opened my house to his friends, knowing it would be safer for them there than out on the street. Children were constantly coming in and out of my apartment. I didn't realize the apartment one floor down was the main headquarters for dope dealing in the neighborhood.

One day, two men came to my door. Only my son and I were in the house at the time. One man forced his way in with a gun in his hand, while the other stood at the door.

The man holding the gun on us told me to give him all of our dope, and when I told him we didn't have any he told us to lay down on the floor. I started screaming, and the man at the door started going around the apartment cutting phone lines and closing the blinds. My son told me to stop screaming then he told them his name.

He said "I'm a high school student. We don't sell drugs here." Around that time, I started praying. I cried out the name of Jesus and they stopped. They moved to go but before they left one man hit my son in the back of the head behind his ear. This type of strike is considered a death blow, but God intervened. My son still has the scar from that blow today.

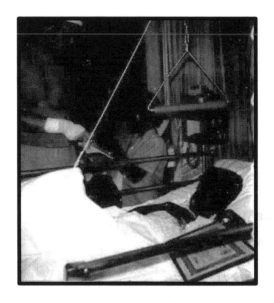

A visit from the Chargers after my boys were
hit by a drunk driver.

CHAPTER ELEVEN

When my second husband started beating me, I had many questions for God. The abuse didn't lessen my love for God, but it did cause me to question His plan for my life. I wanted my marriage to work, not just for me, but for my children, which seems odd when I think about it today. He was neither a good husband nor a good father, but I didn't want to give up on him, because surely God could and would save him if I continued to pray, right?

Wrong. I spent twenty years married to a man I only lived with for two years due to his criminal life and his inability to stay out of jail. Each time he went away my family and I breathed a sigh of relief that he was gone, and regret that he couldn't get it together; that his incarceration didn't rehabilitate him in any way, and that we weren't enough for him to want to turn his life around.

With the Spirit of the Lord in me, I became more vocal at home. I had a boldness that I didn't have before. I became strong enough to file for a divorce. I felt free from the bondage.

I had three children in my two marriages, but never lived with either of the men more than two years in the almost twenty-five years I was married. So, I was on my own raising them. I never thought of myself as being alone; I didn't have anything to judge loneliness by. I had always been alone; it was normal for me. All I knew was that I had to make sure my children were clothed, fed, housed and safe. I didn't have time for much more than that.

In some ways, we all grew up together. I just knew that I was the boss. Hah! They were all such good kids. They were like the sisters and brothers I never had. The only difference was that I knew they depended on me to love, care for, and cherish them forever.

I never talked with my children about what I went through with my husband. I thought and hoped they weren't aware of what was going on.

Now that I look back, there was no way they couldn't know. My husband's abusive behavior wasn't saved just for me. He verbally and mentally abused my children, making his presence in my homeless of a benefit every day and more of a liability to everyone.

I didn't know how all of their lives were affected by my bad choices in husbands, and my staying in situations for so long. I have asked for their forgiveness, and I hope they can forgive me.

CHAPTER TWELVE

My Almost Perfect Job

I loved my job as a counselor. It gave me such hope and purpose. I worked as a counselor for over fifteen years without anyone being the wiser as to what had been going on in my home.

Some of my clients were schizophrenic, while others were bipolar. There were also those who were severely depressed. I loved my job because I felt so much love from my clients and I'm sure they felt love from me.

One of my clients told me that he cut off his penis because he had premarital sex with his girlfriend. He was ashamed of fornicating, he thought his church family would be disappointed in him if they knew that he was having sex. When he told me what he had done, I could hardly believe what I was hearing. We had a full-service building with a psychiatrist, doctors, nurses, and counselors.

My client told me he'd done this to himself years and years ago. He asked me to pray that he became a full man again because he wanted to get married and have children. I prayed with him that very moment. He was a believer in God with mental problems. After he left my office, I went to a nurse who had a connection with one of the larger hospitals in the country. I told her what the client had just told me. She immediately called her doctor friends and told them the story.

Just a few months later the doctors at the hospital wanted to interview my client and do a possible sex organ replacement. One year later he had been fully restored as a man. He and I gave God all the glory.

I took Christian movies to my job site and gave rides to those who wanted to go to church with me. There were even some who gave their lives to Christ during my time at that job.

Just as wonderful as it was to work with my clients, working with some of the staff had me watching behind my back.

The Other side of the Coin

Unfortunately, not every part of my job was wonderful. It happened to ME, TOO!

For the most part, the staff was caring and willing to help. I had a good rapport with just about everyone.

One day I was alone with a staff member in a classroom. At first, we were just talking about how the day was going, but then the subject of conversation took on a very sexual nature. I was shocked and tried to change the subject.

A few moments later other staff members started coming into the room. I was so relieved to be away from that conversation, I didn't even consider telling anyone. Days went by and I didn't think about it anymore. Since we were around each other quite a bit in a group setting, I didn't even think of that person as being any different from what he was before the conversation. I thought he just had an off moment—until the day it happened again.

We were sitting alone in the classroom and he started talking about sex, and what he could do to me and how much he would love to show me what he could do to my body. Again, his vulgar talk was interrupted by other staff members who came into the room. This time I realized that the previous offense wasn't a one-time thing. This man was purposely saying things like that to me, and if I didn't tell someone it would continue. So, I told our supervisor that I was afraid to be alone with him because of his inappropriate conversations. I don't know what she said to him, but it never happened again.

I adored my supervisor. She always looked out for me and the others on staff. When she offered suggestions, we listened because we knew she had our best interest at heart. For some time, my supervisor wanted me to go back to school and get a master's degree. I had finally started divorce proceedings and needed to get away from my ex. I had a B.A. in Behavioral Science, but we both thought that a masters degree would help change my pay scale and also help change some of the politics that were going on at my job. I tried my best to get into a program in my city. I had trouble getting accepted, so after my children graduated from high school I went back to my hometown and was accepted immediately into a Christian psychology program at a graduate school.

Though I was accepted right away, it took me three and a half years to finish grad school because I worked a fulltime job. It usually took two years to finish that course of study. At that point, one of my professor told me that since I was having such a hard time with my studies, I might consider quitting. She said people of my race couldn't complete a curriculum like that, and her reason was that one man like me took her class and he just couldn't make it. I just looked at her, unable to comprehend why she would say such a thing to me. When I got back to my house, I cried all night. I went to my pastor, who was her same race, and asked him why she would say such a thing. He told me she was just testing me to see if I was determined to finish my studies. I accepted his explanation, but I felt she could have challenged me without disparaging my race. I prayed to God that He would help me get through it, and I did. It just so happened that the same teacher that insulted me handed me my lambskin as I crossed the stage during the graduation ceremony. I just looked at her and smiled. It was more than enough to prove her wrong. I was so elated! I couldn't believe I had a Master's in Christian Psychology. I even have a picture of her handing me the diploma that I keep on my wall to this day. It reminds me that no matter what others may say, God has the last word.

My Journey to Being Used

While earning my master's I minored in life coaching. I loved my studies, and I wanted to continue working as a therapist, so I went back to my former job. Unfortunately, the economy had plummeted and there were no positions available for me, and the supervisor that directed me had died. I didn't know what happened or why it happened. I felt hoodwinked, bamboozled; run amuck. I didn't share my feelings with my family because I was usually the strong one, but I was crushed. That year alone I submitted nearly three hundred applications, but I got little to no response. I knew I was more mature in age than most, but I had a great deal to offer. No one looked beyond my age though and I was lost.

I felt a hopelessness in being jobless. I couldn't understand what all of the work God had me do was for. In a sense, I felt betrayed. Nothing seemed to have worked out for all my efforts. I had no money, no job, an empty nest, and no friends that could help. Nothing but God. When I stopped pouting, He gave me hope. He spoke quietly to me to trust Him.

I thought to myself that I would still come back to California to see my kids and grandkids. I still loved the west coast. I floundered and sulked where I was for a little while longer then eventually decided to come back to San Diego and stay. Soon after I arrived in San Diego I attended a women's conference. I was looking for encouragement and inspiration. I ended up talking to a woman about my woes and feelings. When I was done she asked me one question.

"Do you think you have been called to full-time ministry?"

I was instantly transported back to a conversation I'd had with God many years before. I would like to say that I saw what she was inferring, but my first response was denial. I didn't see how He was going to keep me if I was volunteering fulltime. How was I going to survive? I struggled for a little while longer with the decision, but I did pull out old unfinished manuscripts of children's books I'd been holding on to about the God who saved me.

As I slowly embraced the call on my life I began to receive opportunities to speak to young women and serve as a mother of my church. The Lord opened up doors for employment so that I could live on my own. It was a turning point and my life and soul were filled with God.

About two years later I was standing among seven or eight others ministers at the front of the church during morning service to offer prayer to those who needed it. It just so happened that a young lady and her mother got in line to be prayed for. Since they were next in line, once I finished praying with a member they came to me. I believed that moment was ordained by God. I asked the mother what she wanted me to agree with her for. The mother asked me to ask the daughter what she wanted me to pray for. The daughter looked at me and said, "I'm a prostitute and I want God to help me to stop."

I told them that they were standing in front of an ex-prostitute, and I told them to see what God had done for me. The daughter started to cry, and I hugged her and began the prayer of salvation and asked God to give her the power to be released from that bondage. A couple of Sundays later the young girl came to me and gave me a gift to let me know that she was free. It was a tote bag with an angel on it. She had gotten a good job and didn't have to go back out on the street.

Praise God!

My walk with God is very very, very, interesting. I am learning, my thoughts are not at all like God's thoughts. I'm human and He is a spirit and knows all. I know nothing without Him. I am trying to learn how to follow God's will and God's way. I don't get it right all of the time, but it's better than it has been. Living in California has allowed me to feel more connected with the spirit of God. I accepted Him in my hometown in the deep South, but it was the West Coast where I felt the Holy Spirit, which was a whole different experience for me. I can't explain it; I just have faith that the relationship that I have with God now is stronger than ever before. There has been nothing but peace even in the hard times. I am always looking for more of Him. Not more of what I can do or even get, but more of Him in terms of what He wants from me. I know there is more. There is always more.

It was and is a day-to-day choice to trust and lean on Him.

Praying and preaching the word
of our Lord & Savior Jesus Christ

CHAPTER THIRTEEN

Expanding My Borders

I also began to get opportunities to go out of the country. The very last two times I traveled abroad I brought my children's books with me and they became missionary trips. They were marvelous. I've always wanted to do missionary work, and I will go every chance I get.

The Beginning

When my daughter was sent on a book tour to Hawaii for the children's book she wrote she asked me if I wanted to go with her and her kids—my grandkids—I said: "Oh, no thank you." Then I thought, what am I talking about? I said yes, I would love to go.

When I got to Hawaii it was just like everyone said it was. It was so beautiful. The water was so clear and the ocean seemed never ending. I've never seen anything so perfect.

I went with my daughter to the bookstore where she was having one of her book signings. She also read to some of the children at the store. While she was reading, I decided to walk around. I came across a young woman, probably in her early thirties, and said hello. She responded with the same greeting, and I asked her if she knew how Hawaii became part of the United States. I don't know why I led with that question, but the woman seemed eager to give me her view of Hawaii's history and how it became part of the United States.

She said her mother and her aunt still talked about the merge. Her mother told her that the missionaries from the United States came to Hawaii and wanted to convert the natives to their religion. The young woman said that her family was still upset because they wanted to continue their own traditions. At the time I didn't see what that had to do with Hawaii being part of the United States, but the young girl continued to talk about her family losing their traditions. I didn't know how to respond. But I did see that she wanted to talk about her family, so I listened. She seemed relieved to talk to someone about her history.

I mostly listened, but I did ask her, as part of the younger generation of Hawaiians who are making history, how did she feel about the present? She could not answer, so I asked what she was doing to enhance her generation for a better Hawaii. She said that she was in school taking history courses. I assume it was so she could learn more about her ancestors and their beliefs so she could find a way to merge them with the current society and keep them from getting lost forever. She asked me about my history. To me, that was an open window to talk about Jesus. *OMG.*

I told her about how Christianity saved my life. I went on and on about how I believed that Jesus was the Son of God and how my life was not the same since I allowed Him into my heart. She listened with eyes of wonderment. When I finished my testimony, she thanked me for the Good News. I went away thinking that a seed was planted. And I knew the spirit of God would do the rest. I believe that some will plant, others will water. It was a pleasure.

Belize

I first began dreaming of traveling to other countries when I was in high school. Years later, when my friends organized a trip to Belize, I was so excited to finally have the chance to go out of the country. I enjoy seeing other nationalities and love learning about other places. I felt that if I didn't accept this invitation, I would be doing myself a disservice.

The people I traveled with had experience with going abroad, so it was nothing to them, but for me, it was like stepping into another world. The people were marvelous, the food was good, and the town was primitive. The nature hikes were enlightening. Seeing alligators in their natural environment was wonderful and seeing monkeys swinging from tree to tree calling to each other seemed surreal because I had only seen things like that on television. There were so many birds that I had never seen before, and they were all so beautiful. The Caribbean Sea was breathtaking but even after seeing it all in person I was still glad to get back to the United States of America because the mosquitos there were as plentiful as butterflies during springtime in North America. The exception was that butterflies don't suck your blood.

I did go to a school that needed supplies and since I was warned ahead of time that we might come upon such situations, I was prepared to give them some supplies, which had been donated by a nonprofit organization. It was such a wonderful experience; being able to give and pray as we did. One child even accepted the Lord Jesus Christ into his heart. Just being able to be a part of that, was worth the trip.

Puerto Vallarta

A couple of years later I was invited by yet another friend to stay at her timeshare in Puerto Vallarta. The condo was part of a spa resort that was located on the beach. It was the perfect location and I felt years of weariness slide off of me.

Life in a beachfront resort was wonderful. I played "Hold On Old Soldier," on the stereo which made me cry every time I heard it and looked out at the waves from my balcony. I'd asked God for many years to let me experience life on the beach like that, and I did, for six days. *Thank you, Lord.*

Some people said to my face that I wouldn't get the chance to live that dream. Some told me my dreams were too big; that I needed to dream smaller if I actually wanted to see my dreams come true. What they didn't understand was that no dream of mine was too big for God. *Hallelujah!*

Each morning I went out on the balcony and watched the water. The massive ocean just went on and on without end as far as the eye could see. Nothing but blue seas with jungles and mountains on each side. All I could think of was "God is amazing."

It took about three days to absorb the fact that I was there in that area of the world. On that third day when I went outside, tears started to flow out of my eyes. The clouds were heavenly, the sound of the ocean was like angels singing. The weather was super.

I still can't write in words for how I really felt. I was shaking with wonderment. My face couldn't stay dry. I worshiped God with all of my might, with all of my being, and with all of my soul. *God is good.* I also went into tongues, because English was not good enough.

God is my father. Just to think, that ocean had been here for millions and millions of years, since God formed the Earth back in the time of creation.

The world is round and not flat. Men fought to live and explore this world and they have not stopped seeking yet. They have not come close to solving the puzzle of space nor the deep sea, but God is everywhere. He is right here waiting and tugging at our hearts. Without God you would not and could not ever understand how this world could work for you. Without God your understanding is futile.

Since I traveled, I have a better appreciation of His handiwork. God is awesome. I can't give Him enough praise for allowing me in on this secret of His goodness. I know it's been there in the Bible all the time, but now I have a revelation of how magnificent God is just from a human standpoint. It's so much more from a spiritual perspective. I can't even imagine. No let me take that back. My finite mind can't even imagine, but my spirit has glimpsed it.

We went to the ocean to find fish. There were yellow ones and deep, deep blue ones. I was waiting for the dolphins. I heard somewhere that sharks didn't come around the dolphins or vice versa.

We went down into town and saw some of the Mexican people and how they lived. I thought to myself that we had nothing to complain about in the United States. I could see why so many people wanted to run to our country. Our poorest streets were like their richest communities. The people in the town where we were staying were the hardest working people I had ever seen. They weren't standing around begging on the street; they were vendors walking from corner to corner selling food and goods. Tourists were buying their wares so that they could take them home. I was impressed. I was a vendor myself at the time, and I learned so much from the people about how to be persistent, courteous, friendly and serve the client—how to be a good salesperson. God teaches us everything. I went home with a different understanding and new negotiating skills.

CHAPTER FOURTEEN

What Others Take for Granted

As I've shared, I was an extremely shy child and young woman. So much so, that at age sixteen I found that I couldn't recognize words other's my age could. In essence, I could not read. Although I had tutors in the sixth grade, they only helped a little. As school got harder, my concept of reading grew fainter, until I had to find other ways to get by.

At around twenty-five, I asked God for a Holy boldness, and to teach me how to read the Bible. I'm sure it took a few months, but compared to the years I'd tried and failed, it was close to no time before words and comprehension became easy for me. I learned to read by reading the Bible each and every day. It was the first big book I read from beginning to end. I was surprised at how many words I knew.

I asked God for the understanding of His word and He gave it to me. I read with clarity and I understood what God was saying.

I am so thankful for the people who led me to the Lord: first my mother, and then the church who taught me the Bible stories. They were so important to me. I could not read well, but as I grew into the knowledge of who God was, I wanted to know more and more about His will and His way.

Today, my way of giving back and trying to fight against childhood illiteracy is in writing children's books.

I write books for children to help them know Christ at an early age. I am not trying to get rich from my efforts but to get the word out that the sooner you have a relationship with God, the easier it will be for you in life to come.

I write about subjects that will keep them into adulthood, but with the lightheartedness and perspective of a child. I teach them that to listen to a parent is important, but to have a saved parent to listen to is priceless. To read their Bible with understanding is necessary in order to fight off human desires that will harm them in the end. There is an adversary, the devil, who hates God and hates every soul. He is in this

world to keep people from doing the right thing, but God can keep them on the straight and narrow road to His Kingdom for all eternity. Heaven is a place to go to. Hell is a place to avoid. Hell is the place regarded as a spiritual and real realm of evil, filled with suffering that is depicted as a perpetual fire beneath the Earth where the wicked are punished after death. However, heaven is a place above the sky where only the redeemed can live with God forever after they are finished on this Earth.

Writing this book is almost like reliving certain moments of my life. The good ones and the bad ones. I had forgotten some things but it has all come back to me and I can appreciate how God has brought me out.

I now understand the words church mothers speak when they say, "He has brought me from a mighty long way." It's not just a cliché. I really know that God is a deliverer. God saved me from sure damnation and destruction. I don't know how to thank Him but to live for Him and tell others how Jesus saved and rescued me.

In Belize on the mission field witnessing as this child gave his life to Jesus Christ

CHAPTER FIFTEEN

From Generation to Generation

I don't know of too many God-fearing parents who don't want to see their children thrive. Thriving might be too little a word for it. They want to see their children do better, have better and be better than they are. This also pertains to finding favor and having a relationship with God.

They are willing to pray into the early morning over their children, seek God's face on behalf of their children, and praise Him in advance for their health and wellbeing. Even more, they are willing to share with their children what they have witnessed God do for them so that their children will come to understand that not everything is a coincidence.

God Sent a Birth Certificate

The day my daughter, her friend, my granddaughter and I were to leave to go to the Bahamas, my daughter could not find her passport or

113

birth certificate. We still got on a plane in hopes that we could still somehow board the ship once we landed. We got to Florida, and by then we were thinking of different ways we might be able to get a birth certificate so she could still get on the ship with us. I started praying, *Lord we need your help.*

My daughter started calling old employers and schools that might have a copy of her birth certificate. She even called a friend to go to the county clerk's office and buy a birth certificate and fax it to her. One hour before we were to board the ship, she had called about ten to twenty people, thinking that she would miss the trip and all of her plans would fly out the window. She even told us that we could go ahead, and she would just fly back home.

Just as boarding began, her phone rang. The person on the other end said they had her birth certificate, and they were wanting to know where to fax it. She went to a courtesy area at the airport and had the birth certificate faxed to that number. And we were all able to go on the trip. *Praise God. He is so good*

Prayer Does Change Things

One day, when my daughter came home from work, she went to check the mail as always. When she stopped at the mailbox, she bent over in pain, then fell to her knees on the sidewalk, unable to move. One of her neighbors saw her and went to his home and got a wheelchair. He wheeled her to her apartment, where she called a nurse that served in her healthcare medical group. The nurse told her to put an ice pack on the area of her lower back where she was feeling the most pain.

An hour later the pain was worse, and she could not stand or move. She called the nurse back and told her that the pain had escalated. The nurse called an ambulance for her. They rolled the gurney to her apartment and lowered it to the floor. She rolled over onto it, still in a great deal of pain. When she got to the emergency room the doctor sent her through many types of tests. She was sent home, with the doctor telling her that she had a degenerative bone disease and there was nothing they could do for her.

For three days my daughter laid still with her fourteen-year-old son helping her to the bathroom. She crawled and scooted along the floor trying to get around. At the end of the third day, I came to her apartment with a two-handled walker and we prayed. She stood up and began to walk. I screamed with joy saying, "You can walk!"

I took her straight to her primary care doctor. We were looking for another opinion from what the emergency doctor told her. We didn't believe that there was nothing that they could do nor that she would have to live with the degenerative bone disease in such a manner for the rest of her life. When we got to the primary care's office the doctor checked and said the disease had reversed. My daughter and I looked at each other and started crying with joy. She went back to work the next day. God is wonderful!

Learning from the Past

Even when we are not present, God is always faithful and just to take care of those we have been praying over. There are many instances over the years that my children have shared with me that have me bursting into tears because I am thankful that God kept them safe even without my knowledge.

My son just recently told me that when he was young, he drove into a lake and couldn't manage to swim to the top. He said he felt something pull both his arms up until he saw the top of the water. He didn't know how or who pulled him up, but I know.

When my other son was in his forties, he asked me why I took him away from his family and my hometown when he was only three years old. I was shocked to hear him ask that question. I thought he knew that we didn't have any family in the area anymore. By the time he was three, both of my parents were deceased, and I wasn't close with my extended family from my father's first marriage.

117

My son did go back to our hometown one year, but there was no one there from our family. He said that the city had gone back in time. The streetlights looked like they were hanging on strings or clotheslines.

He seemed very disappointed in where he was born, but I wanted him to know that the history lesson wasn't to make him feel less about himself. It was to help him understand all of the challenges he'd overcome to get to the place he was today. We can't choose where we are born and what family we are born into.

What I didn't share with him was that the town had been influenced by Jim Crow Laws. That I didn't want to see any of my children hanging from the bridge he crossed to get into my old neighborhood. I also didn't tell him that I couldn't imagine subjecting him or any of my other children to a life that only offered work at a Foundry, which had slowly killed their grandfather. In that instance I could do something to save my children and God in His

118

infinite grace and mercy gave me the mindset, finances, and support to do so.

We can't pick our privileges. We can only decide and work toward realizing the goals we have set for ourselves, both in the natural and spiritual world.

PROMISES KEPT

My Guardian Angel

One night I went to bed after taking my usual medication. I was sleeping soundly, but I had a very strange dream. I was asleep, but I could also see outside of my body. I saw an angel trying to wake me up. I was in such a deep and peaceful sleep that I didn't want to wake up, but whatever was trying to wake me was relentless. It seemed like the angel was trying to shake me awake, and I finally came out of my sleep with a jolt. When the angel was finally able to wake me up I realized I was having diabetic tremors and was on the verge of going into shock.

119

It seemed as though I had taken too much medication. I was able to get up to reverse the condition by bringing my blood sugar back up. If the angel had not been successful, I would have died in my sleep.

CHAPTER SIXTEEN

These Years of Restoration

I find myself enjoying my later years. I call them my "years of restoration," because my prior years were so challenging and unpredictable. I am enjoying sharing my legacy with my grandkids. I am happy and content with who I am. I am loving the freedom that comes with retirement.

Throughout my early life, the days were unsure and perplexing. I would wake up in fear that I would not measure up to my mother's expectations or gain the knowledge to be able to express myself properly, let alone take care of myself. Fear gripped my young life for years. The old saying "out of the frying pan into the fire" was also part of my life, as my marriages were worse than my childhood life.

After the marriages, which took up a great deal of my young life, I just knew I needed to get a good education.

Though I was an older adult when I entered college the second time, I believed my degree would make my professional life easier and allow me to gain more money in the field that I loved. Not so.

I got out of college with my master's degree just in time for the economic market to crash. What was a mature woman to do? I wasn't sure what God was trying to show me. It was hard to see His hand in my life. And the depression I faced from feeling like a failure and not knowing where to go didn't make it easier for me to hear Him.

So, I moved into a retirement facility thinking, *what is happening to me, and most of all, what steps do I take now?*

What steps are in my plans for my future? How will I support myself? How will I feed myself? How can I live a guilt-free life and not allow the things I did in my past to cause me to doubt my worth?

I had a specific idea of what being a college graduate, a church-going Christian, and a single mother who raised three children alone should look like, and this wasn't it.

I wondered where I went wrong. I had an unsettling in my spirit which made be restless, anxious, and bored.

Since I had gone to school and earned a master's in psychology, I decided to counsel myself. *Lord help me conquer these ungodly feelings of defeat.*

I went to New York to visit a friend. We went to a beach, and I saw shells just lying on the sand. I picked up all of the shells I could find and started towards my journey in jewelry making. I made necklaces, earrings, and bracelets from seashells.

The unrest ceased and the anxiety lessened; the boredom was replaced with activity. When I think about those years when I was in between doing what I thought I should do and knowing what I should do I am thankful to have come out on the other side and humbled by God giving yet another gift that would remind me of the desire He put in my heart so long ago. The ocean called as it had when I was young.

After finding out that I could make things with my hands I began to enjoy the new journey. I thought to myself, *what else can I do that I never thought I could do*? All the while I was working on getting my body back into a healthier form and trying to drink and eat healthier.

I came across my Frugal Fruit characters around the same time. These fruity characters filled with Biblical and nutritional knowledge had been sitting in my closet for years. Ms. Strawberry, Mr. Pear, Mrs. Plum, and Little Miss Grapes. Along with them I found my book on where dinosaurs came from. My nephew. David Adams drew the illustrated characters of the dinosaurs and different fruit groups to put in a short storybook for kids and the kids at heart.

The Frugal Fruit Family and Friends concept was developed so that children could learn while at play. I wanted an enthusiastic and compassionate book for children to engage in, that would train them to express their knowledge of Christian and community

124

concerns for their past and future. I wanted to place a book in every child's hand in the community, and eventually the whole wide world.

I wanted these books to be a legacy for parents to leave for their children and grandchildren, to help them learn and express their natural God-given creativity and talent. It's so important for children to be physically fit, mentally clear and spiritually aware for the future. When I started writing these books, I saw that my journey was not in vain. I love creating each short story. It gives me great joy to share what I have learned. To be able to pass it on to anyone who is in need of some kind of hope and freedom in their life.

You may think kids are not watching, listening, or caring about their futures but they are. They need parents, teachers, and educators to prepare their minds for the best possible outcome for what is to come.

Today I am still learning; I am still asking the Lord, "what do you have for me to do? What can I do to please you, without adding my own understanding about what I think I am here for? "Lord lead me and guide me, so that I may guide someone else into a lifestyle of peace and honor." I have joy and peace, and it all comes from sitting quietly enough to hear the Lord, and then doing what He says.

The flow of His words is contagious, inspiring and comforting. I believe Romans 8:28 and we know that all things work together for the good to them that love God, to them who are the called according to His purpose. I love His promises and I believe Isaiah 65:24 "And it shall come to pass that before they call, I will answer, and while they are yet speaking, I will hear.

As I draw closer to the end of this book, I am excited to see what is next in my life, and what I will discover. I play relaxing music while I write, and the flow of words just comes out of my mind and down to my fingers. Thoughts of peace, love, and happiness. The peace of wellness and calmness flows from my body like you can't possibly understand.

I was sitting in my doctor's waiting room one day. I was on time and I expected my doctor to be ready to see me, but don't you know, he wasn't. I started an old routine of anxiety and unrest. Then I dug through my purse and saw my writing pad. I looked and looked again for a pen or pencil and found my favorite ink pen. I started writing and writing, and then I came up with a new title for a new book. I thought, *wow it works*. All the anxiety and unrest left and was replaced with creativity. When the doctor came in, he said, "Wow what a great past time!" I smiled and thought, *you just don't know*.

Then there are those days…

There are still days I feel drained, and it's all I can do to hold back the tears of defeat and despair. I feel helpless and hopeless. I can't even tell you why this spirit of depression comes over me on occasion. But it is those times that remind me of the strength of God in my weakness. Since it doesn't happen often, I find that when it does, I want to record it in my mind, so it has less of a chance of sneaking up on me. I take note of the feelings that lead to depression and what I might have been doing or thinking the day before. I try to make sure I don't indulge in defeated thinking and give myself pity parties.

There is one depressive episode in particular that I remember very well, just due to the conversations it evoked.

I was so surprised because I usually felt so upbeat. I love to smile and play, but that day grabbed me and took ahold of my mind, body, and soul. I was totally under something that I did not understand. I did not tell anyone of the depths of depression that I felt because I felt that no one could help me. And if they could help, me they wouldn't care to. I felt that they would not believe me because I was always so upbeat.

I did mention it to one person, and they told me, "I can't believe you need help, you have always been so independent and carefree."

I went back to my home and cried and cried and cried. I said out loud, "Lord, I have no one but you, please help me overcome this debilitating depression." I had always wondered how comedians could kill themselves. At that moment I understand how it could happen.

Please, Lord, take this depression and hopelessness away from me.

One night, while I was sitting up in bed, I put gospel music on a loop and went into a very deep sleep. I don't remember dreaming which is odd because I know I dream a lot even though I may not remember what I dream.

I woke up several hours later; about seven or out eight hours later. It was the next day. I searched and searched in my mind for that thing that had me bound the prior two days. The thing that had me crying and feeling pitiful, and had me trying to think of a way to destroy myself and my soul. It was gone.

Hallelujah!

I could think clearly and positively again. I was back to my old self again. I felt refreshed and calm; no depression, no anger. The tears came, but they were tears of joy, and not of defeat and shame. They were tears of being glad to be alive. They were tears set amongst the thoughts that I was beautiful.

Although that depressive state lasted only a couple of days, it felt like a lifetime of misery. I am not going to say it will never happen again, but I will say I will immediately know when it tries to enter into my space and confuse my mind. I will call on the name of Jesus and he will deliver me from all hurt, harm, and danger. I know that that is not just a cliché, but a fact.

The devil is real, but God has defeated him for our sake. Thank you, Jesus. I give God all the honor and praise. Without God I know I would be lost.

Without God, my soul would be condemned to the pit of hell.

Without God, I could do nothing but fail, as the song says. With God I have a future. With God my mind is clear and bright. With God I have a chance for eternal life with Him on high. He saved me, gave me three wonderful children, a place to stay and food to eat. With God my whole life changed for the better.

Now during the years of restoration, I can see how God was with me all the time. I know I have made some very bad choices and bad moves, but God refused to let me go. He just kept blessing me over and over again. I try so hard to be good and thankful because I don't want to disappoint my God, but sometimes I still catch myself thinking and even doing the wrong things. I know God would not approve of these things and I say, "Lord, help my way of thinking. Lord, help my unbelief. Lord, help my lack of faith. Lord help me."

I am a work unfinished. This book is part of my restoration. This book has unraveled and untwisted thoughts in my mind. This book will help start a new day. It gives a new meaning to being born again. I still have hurt, shame, common guilt and shyness in me but I am coming out of that. I can begin to be free from the pain of living.

Without God, who saw me through all of it, I would not be here telling this story. I still play the songs "Hold On Old Soldier and Your Grace and Mercy Brought me Through every morning to revive myself and let God know how grateful I am for Him keeping me, and for saving me and protecting me from hell, and myself. Now I go all over the world preaching and teaching about the love of God.

Hallelujah!

My wonderful Professors wishing me well
at my graduate school ceremony.

CHAPTER SEVENTEEN

What Were You Born For?

You were born to be successful. Your fighting spirit goes way beyond the boundaries of this world, and someday all of your hard work will pay off.

This book has given me the freedom to remember the past without guilt or shame. I feel free, clear and clean of secrets. My mind is going on a fishing trip for answers. As a child I felt restricted, boxed-in, smothered, and insignificant. I had no self-worth, low self-esteem, and an incredible shyness, to the point where the thought of talking to someone would make me tremble.

I'm starting to open up, speak my mind and look people in their eyes, knowing that the shyness is lifting. I didn't know how good it would feel to wake up in the morning free from fear.

Just before one of my relatives passed away, he said that he was glad he'd gotten to know me as an adult since I was so quiet as a child.

Growing up in the background and in the shadows is a lonely place. After knowing God as my personal Savior I have been able to take some of the boldness that He has given me to open up a brand new life for me. Sometimes I can't believe it is me I am looking at in the mirror. When I talk it surprises me to hear what comes out of my mouth. Now it's exciting to be with my friends because I have something to contribute to the conversation. When it's time to go to church I not only love the word of God but I love to meet with God's people who used to make me shake in fear.

I asked God for holy boldness so that I was not so afraid of people. Talking to them wasn't really the problem. I just never thought I had anything worthwhile to talk about. I didn't just want to throw out words or have a meaningless conversation with people.

Now I have learned that I can have meaningful conversations and say words that make a difference. I also love to listen. It's my specialty. I feel most comfortable sitting and listening, but now I know when it's my turn to talk, and I can say what I need to say. I was perfect for the profession that God chose for me. Even retired, I still find ways to use what He provided me to learn.

At this point in time, my sole purpose is to love the Lord and give thanks to Him who died on the cross for me. There is no greater love than who would send His only begotten son for my sake.

As I write this book, I am reminded what all God has done for me. Even at an early age, He has been with me all the time. I am so glad I know the sacrifice my Lord has made for me and who is still praying on my behalf.

Sometimes it is hard to contain myself without yelling out loud, "Thank you!" Lord! I hear His voice, I see His miracles, I know what he wants. Most of the time and I do my best to succumb to His wishes. Loving God is so easy for me because not only did he first love me, but He had never stopped loving me. I am His Girl! He is my Father!

I am excited. I am a witness to tell the world that this world is only a stage to get ready for the main

attraction. Heaven will be my home and I'm glad about it. Today is a good day to talk about our ever-lasting home. What will be your lasting place? Let Jesus be your guide. No matter what has happened to you, God loves you and only wants the best for you and yours. "Be Blessed."

One of the biggest dreams I've had, came true earlier this year when my newly released children's book 'Castles in the Sand' became a #1 New Release on Amazon in the Children's Books category.

It's one of the achievements in my life that have made me proud. Here are a few others.

New Alternatives CATC
4307 Third Avenue
San Diego, CA. 92103

To Whom It May Concern:

It is my pleasure to write this recommendation on Barbara Patmon whom I have known for the past ten months at New Alternatives CATC. I have worked as a licensed clinical social worker and supervisor of National University interns and staff who want to accumulate hours for their Marriage, Family and Child Counselor license. Barbara approached me in April to supervise her for her hours and we began meeting.

I have observed Barbara grow from a reticent, quiet child care staff person to one who has gained self-confidence and who is assertive. She actively participates in our in-service education programs.

Since we have shared several female clients together, I have observed first hand her interaction with them. I believe she is a caring person, one who has good assessment skills, that is, she can "size up" a person and set objectives for them to help them grow. The young people here must agree to a weekly contract that is often arrived at conjointly. I note that Barbara has selected significant aspects of a child's personality or behavior to work on through the contract.

I have found Barbara to be a decisive, reliable and low-keyed person. I have a great deal of respect for this woman who went to college and held a full time job while raising three children alone.

I write this letter of recommendation knowing full well Barbara's departure from CATC would be a great loss.

Sincerely yours,

Jeanne A. Gill

Jeanne A. Gill, LCSW, Ph.D.

139

Fortwood Center Inc.

Presents

This Certificate of Recognition To

BARBARA MODENA

For Compliments Received From Our Customer Survey

2/4/05
Date

Jun Mudly
Signature

142

Certificate of Attendance

Presented To

Barbara Modena

For attending the
60-hour Office of Emergency Services Approved
Domestic Violence and Sexual Assault Crisis Intervention Training,
March 2009
CENTER FOR COMMUNITY SOLUTIONS San Diego, California

Danielle Lingle, Associate Executive Director

Nelly Gregorian DeLeon, Director of Counseling Services

Team Player Award

In honor of your
outstanding performance and
dedication
we hereby present
Barbara Modena
with this certificate of recognition for
your high standards of excellence
at Family Foundations Program
San Diego

You Are A Star!

Awarded On: August 5, 2008
Presented By: _____
Tracy Wells, CADC II
Program Director

✷ ✷ ✷ ✷ ✷

NATIONAL UNIVERSITY

Be it known that the Board of Trustees,
upon recommendation of the Faculty,
has conferred the Degree

BACHELOR OF ARTS
IN BEHAVIORAL SCIENCE

with all Responsibilities, Rights, and
Privileges pertaining, upon

BARBARA S. PATMON

In testimony whereof, having demonstrated
to the Faculty the High Level of
Competence, this Diploma is granted.

Given at San Diego, California, this
Tenth day of April, in the
year of our Lord 1983.

FORTWOOD CENTER, INC.

Providing Quality
Mental Health Services
to Chattanooga

Oct. 31, 2005
Date

Dear Ms. Modena

On behalf of Fortwood Center's Supervised System of Care, and in conjunction with our Credentialing Review Committee, it is my pleasure to inform you that your application has been reviewed and approved as meeting the required recredentialing criteria.

In order to continue meeting credentialing criteria, it is **your responsibility** to assure that copies of your current license(s) and/or certification(s) are provided before or at the date of expiration to Joan Rollins at the Main Center. Also, it is **your responsibility** to provide Sandy Swanson in the Human Resources Department copies of special training and continuing education that you participate in throughout the year.

Termination of employment will result in immediate rescission of credentialing privileges with Fortwood Center, Inc.

If you have any questions, please feel free to call.

Sincerely,

Dorothy Stephens LSPE
Fortwood Center, Inc.
Supervised System of Care

jr

1028 East Third Street • Chattanooga, Tennessee 37403 • (423) 266-6751 • Fax (423) 763-4650

Equal Opportunity Employer
A United Way Agency

Diploma

Be it known that _____ BARBARA PAYNON

has successfully completed the course of instruction in

_____ JOB SEARCH WORKSHOP _____

administered through the

_____ WIN EMPLOYMENT PREPARATION PROGRAM _____

Awarded this 11TH day of MARCH

in the year of 1987

Signed _____

Title _____ EPA SUPERVISOR

JOB SERVICE

Certificate of
ATTENDANCE
Stress Solutions Workshop for Women™

An ETC ®/CareerTrack seminar

Barbara S. Modena
Signature of Seminar Participant

Sept. 4, 1997
Date

John Ball, Vice President,
Marketing & Development

3085 Center Green Drive
Boulder, CO U.S.A. 80301-5408
(303) 440-7440
http://www.careertrack.com

State of Tennessee
Certificate

TENNESSEE STATE BOARD FOR VOCATIONAL EDUCATION

This is to certify that   BARBARA SUE PATMON   has completed 439 hours of instruction in   KEYPUNCH OPERATOR   under provisions of the State Plan for Vocational-Technical Education.

Conducted by   STATE AREA VOCATIONAL - TECHNICAL SCHOOL

located at   CHATTANOOGA   , Tennessee, from   04/29/74   to   09/16/74.

In testimony of this fact we have hereunto affixed our signatures this the 16th day of SEPTEMBER, 19 74.

Ralph B. Mitchell
Superintendent Area Vocational-Technical School

W. M. Harrison
Assistant Commissioner
Vocational-Technical Education

W. M. Jackson, Jr.
Coordinator
Area Vocational-Technical School

Benjamin E. Carmichael
Executive Officer
State Board For Vocational Education

Psychological Studies Institute

On recommendation of the Faculty
and by authority of the Board of Trustees,
Psychological Studies Institute hereby confers upon

Barbara Modena

the degree of

Master of Science in Christian Psychological Studies

Specialization in Leadership and Coaching

with all the rights, privileges, and distinctions pertaining thereto.

This twelfth day of May, in the year of our Lord, 2007.

_____
President

_____
Chairman of the Board of Trustees

THE NEIGHBORHOOD HOUSE ASSOCIATION

PROJECT ENABLE CCTC
266 Euclid Avenue · Suite 102 · San Diego, CA 92114 · 263-6155 Ext. 100

CHAIRMAN
James E. Hatcher

PRESIDENT / CEO
Howard H. Carey, Ph.D.

June 05, 1996

TO WHOM IT MAY CONCERN

Components

Day Treatment
263-6155

Socialization
263-6269

Vocational Services
266-9400

Medication Mgmt.
266-2111

Outpatient
266-9881

Project Enable-Socialization is a non-profit social rehabilitation program for the mentally disabled run by the Neighborhood House Association.

Ms. Barbara Patmon-Modena has been working for the Neighborhood House Association Project Enable from August 13, 1989 until June 05, 1996 as a Socialization Counselor.

Ms. Modena's duties included intake and admission of new clients, developing individual service plans, providing her clients with guidance and assistance to implement the service plans which focus on enhancing their social, independent living, symptom management and physical skills, driving the program van during outings, and leading group sessions and work units.

Besides successfully carrying out the afore-mentioned duties, Ms. Modena has demonstrated extra-ordinary interest and skill in helping clients acquire emotional encouragement and maintain proper grooming and personal hygiene. She has been cooperative and willing to work in collaboration with the other staff members and myself for the benefit of maximizing the quality of the program output.

I wish Ms. Modena success in her future endeavors.

Ayele H. Mclkte
Socialization Coordinator

United Way
of San Diego County

A member of the United Way, The United Neighborhood Centers of America and A Delegate Agency of the Community Action Program.

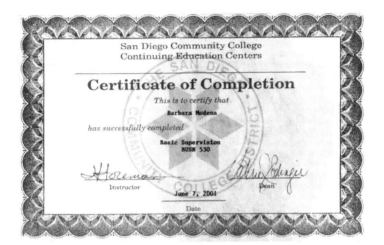

San Diego Community College
Continuing Education Centers

Certificate of Completion

This is to certify that

Barbara Modena

has successfully completed

Basic Supervision
BUSN 530

_____
Instructor

June 7, 2001
Date

_____
Dean

National Center for Housing Management
Certified Manager of Housing

This certifies that

Barbara Modena

*has successfully completed the course of study and
passed the examination on housing management
and procedures and has met the standards for certification
provided by the National Center for Housing Management*

00102132
Id. Number

Chairman

President

3/24/98
Date

ABOUT THE AUTHOR

Barbara Sue Modena was born and raised in Tennessee. She lived in an era full of promise but filled with short-sightedness when it came to young black women in the South.

Barbara Modena has a love for people, especially children, and the ocean, no matter which side of the country she's on. The Pacific Ocean and the need to spread her wings drew her to California, where she currently resides.

After being diagnosed with diabetes, Barbara studied ways to make her diet both flavorful and healthy. Inspired by what she learned, she searched for a way to teach children about both physical and spiritual nutrition in a way that was fun and engaging. She began writing children's books in 2008 and has never looked back.

Barbara fills her days serving God any way she can, whether writing, crafting, serving as a minister and mother of her church, or providing crisis counseling.

Barbara S. Modena's Books Ready for Purchase

Names of God

Books of the Bible

Fruits of the Spirit

Why Go to Church

God is One

God's Seven Churches from Revelations

Creation

The Good Samaritan

How can I Live with Jesus Forever?

Frugal Fruit Family & Friends Coloring Books

Frugal Fruit and the Dinosaurs

What Does the Bible say about Nutrition?

Frugal Fruit Go to the Dentist

Frugal Fruit Teaches Kids about Heaven or Hell

Castles in the Sand: Where is Heaven

My Skin is Brown

53486908R00085

Made in the
USA
Lexington, KY